To

_____

On the occasion of

_____

From

_____

Date

GW00370868

Published by
Lion Publishing plc
Sandy Lane West, Oxford, England
ISBN 0 7459 1223 0 (gift edition)
ISBN 0 7459 1535 3

Lion Publishing Corporation
1705 Hubbard Avenue, Batavia, Illinois 60510, USA
ISBN 0 7459 1223 0 (gift edition)
ISBN 0 7459 1535 3

Albatross Books Pty Ltd
PO Box 320, Sutherland, NSW 2232, Australia
ISBN 0 86760 886 2

First edition 1987
Reprinted 1988, 1990

Illustrations by Chris Barker

Printed and bound in Italy

MARION STROUD

O·U·R
FAMILY

A LION BOOK

Oxford · Batavia · Sydney

CONTENTS

People need people! From birth to death there is implanted in each of us an inescapable need to belong, to be special to someone; to have our own place in the overall scheme of things. God himself made us this way: we are designed to live in families.

A family begins with two people who love one another. Out of their love, children are born and something new comes into being. A small thing at first, but rapidly growing and altering in shape and style and identity as different personalities join to form an ever-changing tapestry of intertwining lives.

Sometimes the tapestry of family life carries dark threads woven into the warp and weft of loving and belonging. Gaps and frayed edges appear, weakening the whole fabric. And in the hectic pace of late twentieth-century living we can easily lose sight of the whole pattern because we forget, drift apart, become separated by time and distance. So this book is intended to act as a reminder. A reminder that people matter. That we all have something to offer one another. That the past and the present hold hands with the future. And that God intends human families to reflect, however imperfectly, his love and fatherly care for everyone.

Marion Stroud

A PORTRAIT

The way we look,
  our hopes and fears
Lessons we've learned
  throughout the years.
The things we've done,
  the places seen
The goals achieved,
  the 'might have been'.
The truths on which
  our life has stood
The faith we'd give
  you if we could.

His name

Date of birth

Place of birth

Education

Occupation

Date of marriage

Countries visited

Things that are important to me

How I would like to be remembered

Her name

Date of birth

Place of birth

Education

Occupation

Date of marriage

Countries visited

Things that are important to me

How I would like to be remembered

Photograph

Photograph

R O O T S

Father _____

Husband _____ 15

Mother _____

1 _____ Great Grandfather
                          9 _____ Grandfather
2 _____ Great Grandmother

3 _____ Great Grandfather
                          10 _____ Grandmother
4 _____ Great Grandmother

5 _____ Great Grandfather
                          11 _____ Grandfather
6 _____ Great Grandmother

7 _____ Great Grandfather
                          12 _____ Grandmother
8 _____ Great Grandmother

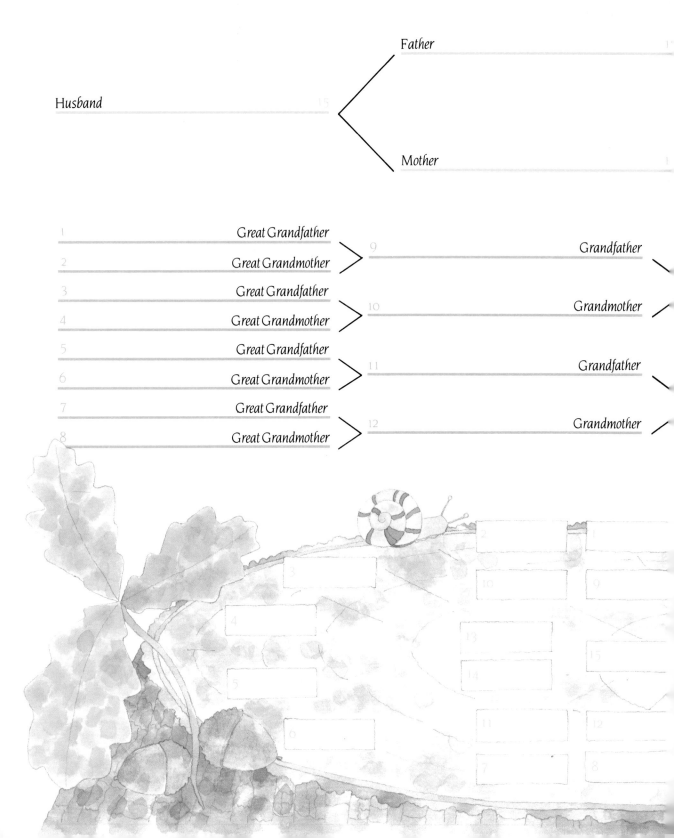

Grandfather _____

Great Grandfather _____
Great Grandmother _____

Grandmother _____

Great Grandfather _____
Great Grandmother _____

Grandfather _____

Great Grandfather _____
Great Grandmother _____

Grandmother _____

Great Grandfather _____
Great Grandmother _____

_____ Father

15 _____ Wife

_____ Mother

Fill in dates of birth

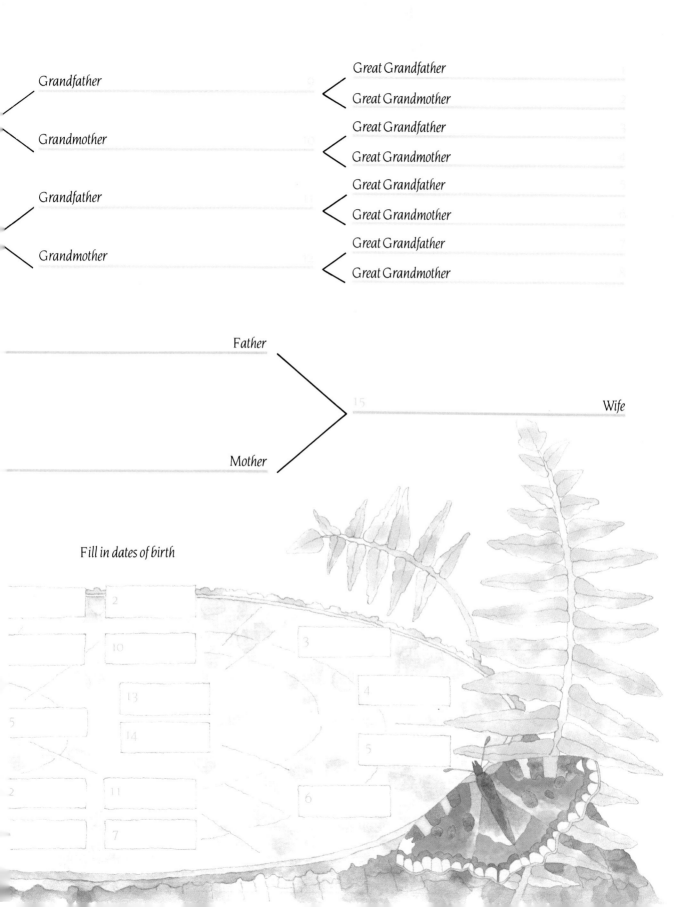

When our roots go down
deeply into the love
and faithfulness of God,
We can accept the past
with thankfulness,
Enjoy the present
without fear
And move into the future
with confidence.

Name and age

Relationship

Date of photograph

Occasion

Name and age

Relationship

Date of photograph

Occasion

Name and age

Relationship

Date of photograph

Occasion

Name and age

Relationship

Date of photograph

Occasion

Old Family Photographs

It is so easy to feel
Both small and insignificant,
Having no purpose
In the overall scheme
  of things.
And yet in God's eyes
There are no nonentities.
Each life is given
At just the right time
To do and to be
Something special and
  irreplaceable.
For you and I are
  lovingly shaped
To be the building blocks
From which history is created.

'I ask that work should be looked upon not as a necessary drudgery to be undergone for the purpose of making money, but as a way of life in which the nature of man should find its proper exercise and delight and so fulfil itself to the glory of God.' *Dorothy L. Sayers*

Name

Name

Name

Name

Name

Name

Name

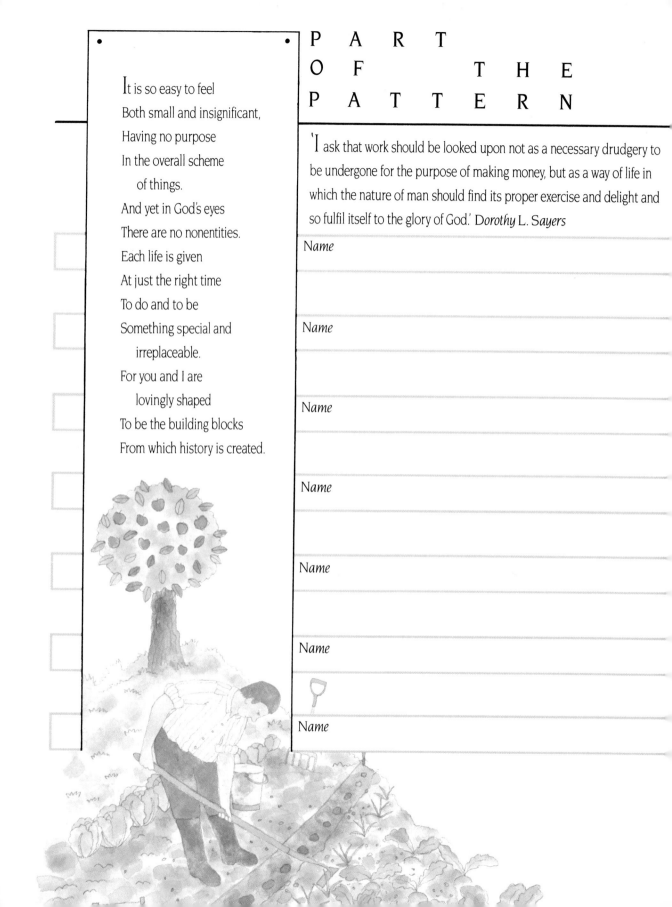

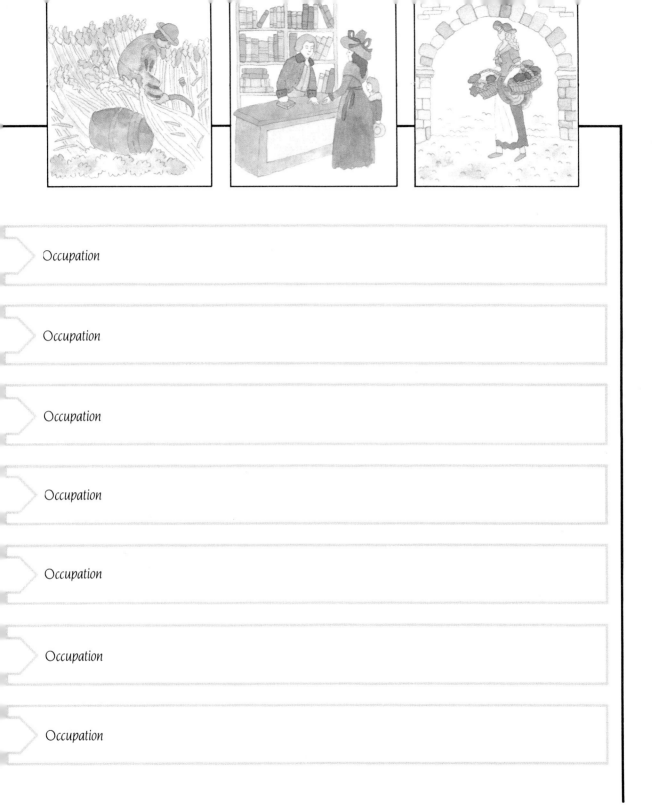

Occupation

Occupation

Occupation

Occupation

Occupation

Occupation

Occupation

How times have changed!
Different clothes, different jobs,
Different pastimes,
   different manners.
Children definitely heard,
Although, once past a certain age
Seldom seen.

The world appears smaller
Because transport moves faster
And legs (for walking with)
Seem almost out of fashion.

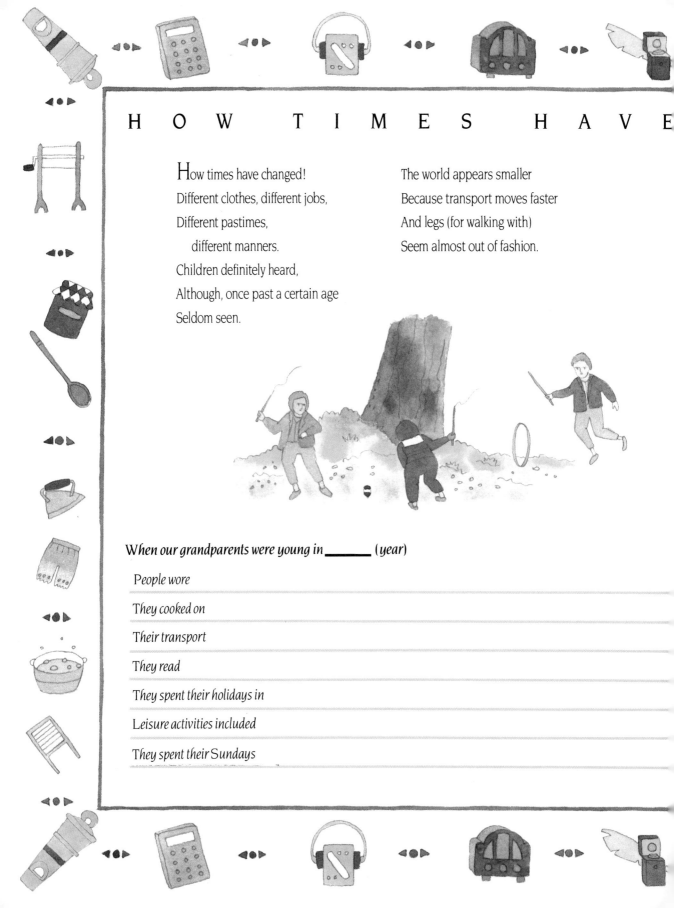

When our grandparents were young in _____ (year)

People wore

They cooked on

Their transport

They read

They spent their holidays in

Leisure activities included

They spent their Sundays

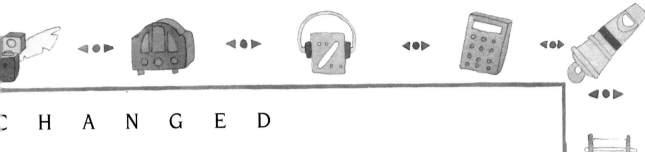

C H A N G E D

We grapple with new pressure
  and new problems
As well as possibilities
  once only dreamed about.
And yet...underneath...
  people stay the same.

We have the same need
  for love and laughter,
Caring and commitment.
We still need to know beneath us
The Rock of truth and trust,
And all around the comfort of
  God's everlasting arms.

Life in _____ (year) is a little different

Current fashions include

We cook on

Our transport

We enjoy authors such as

We spend our holidays

Our leisure activities include

Sunday is the day when

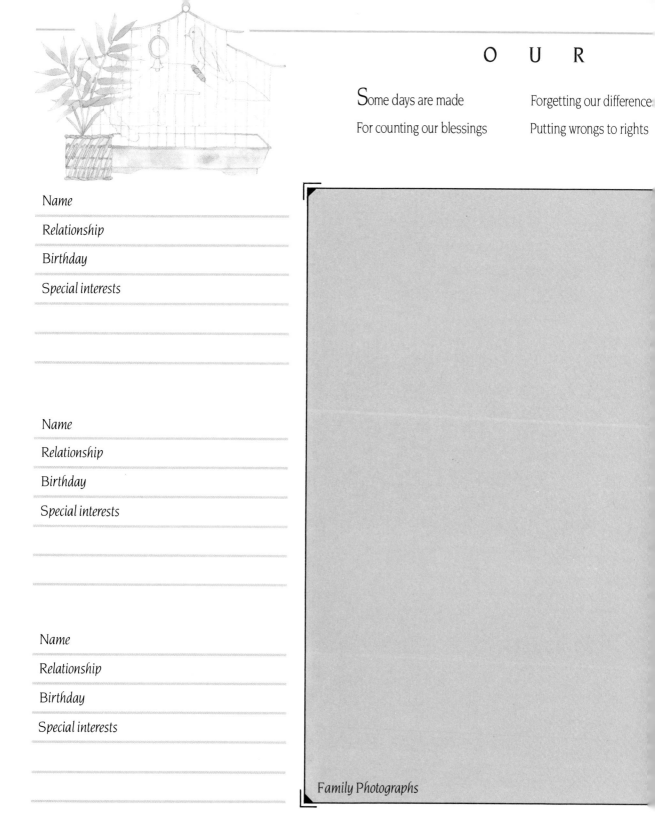

Some days are made

For counting our blessings

Forgetting our differences

Putting wrongs to rights

Name
_____

Relationship
_____

Birthday
_____

Special interests
_____

_____

_____

Name
_____

Relationship
_____

Birthday
_____

Special interests
_____

_____

_____

Name
_____

Relationship
_____

Birthday
_____

Special interests
_____

_____

_____

Family Photographs

M I L Y

olding out a hand and saying   That we are a family.'

love you and I'm glad   Today is such a day.

Name

Relationship

Birthday

Special interests

Name

Relationship

Birthday

Special interests

Name

Relationship

Birthday

Special interests

There was no way to guess when we first met you,

That God had sent you to us to become

Not simply friends but truly 'family'

Bonded by love, not just by blood or obligation

To be a vital glowing segment

In the patchwork of our lives.

Name

Date of birth

Special memories

Name

Date of birth

Special memories

Name

Date of birth

Special memories

Name

Date of birth

Special memories

Name

Date of birth

Special memories

F A M I L Y

Name

Date of birth

Special memories

Name

Date of birth

Special memories

Name

Date of birth

Special memories

Name

Date of birth

Special memories

Family Photographs

H O M E　　　　　S W E E T

His Granny's house

Name
_____

Address
_____
_____

What I remember
_____
_____
_____
_____
_____

His childhood home

Address
_____
_____

When I lived there
_____

What I liked about our home
_____
_____

The people next door were
_____

What I remember about them
_____
_____
_____

Her Granny's house

Name
_____

Address
_____

What I remember
_____
_____
_____
_____

Her childhood home

Address
_____
_____

When I lived there
_____

What I liked about our home
_____
_____

The people next door were
_____

What I remember about them
_____

H O M E

His childhood home

Address

_____

_____

When I lived there

What I liked about our home

_____

_____

_____

The people next door were

What I remember about them

_____

_____

_____

_____

Her childhood home

Address

_____

_____

When I lived there

What I liked about our home

_____

_____

_____

The people next door were

What I remember about them

_____

_____

_____

23

Looking at them,
Without the eyes of love,
They may not all have
        seemed to be
Desirable residences.
But ordinary although
        they may appear,
Difficult to run, perhaps,
        to get to or to pay for,
For us they have been home.
These are the walls that
        kept our family safe,
Saw our tears and heard
        our laughter.
Within their shelter we
        have learned
To love and live with others.
And here we have been able
To be ourselves,
        relaxed, at ease,
Protected at least
        in some small measure,
From all the pain and pressures
        of the world outside.

H O M E   S W E E T   H O M E

Our first home together

Address

When we lived there

What was special about it

Other homes

Address

When we lived there

What was special about it

Address

When we lived there

What was special about it

Address

When we lived there

What was special about it

M E A L T I M E S

For health and strength and daily food
We give you thanks, O Lord.

Our family grace

_____

_____

_____

_____

_____

Childhood mealtimes

Foods we had as children

_____

_____

Puddings we liked best

_____

_____

Special food at parties included

_____

_____

Name

Likes

Dislikes

Name

Likes

Dislikes

Name

Likes

Dislikes

Name

Likes

Dislikes

Name

Likes

Dislikes

Name

Likes

Dislikes

His schools

Name	Dates
Name	Dates
Name	Dates
Name	Dates

What I wore to school

Special friends

Teachers I remember

Amusing incidents at school

Classic comments on school reports

'Always remember what you have learned. Your education is your life. Guard it well.' *From Proverbs, chapter 4*

Her schools

Name   Dates

Name   Dates

Name   Dates

Name   Dates

What I wore to school

Special friends

Teachers I remember

Amusing incidents at school

Classic comments on school reports

Photograph

Holidays where everything went wrong!

Places we have visited together

Places we have stayed together

Other special times we'd like to remember

Photograph

OUR HOLIDAYS

These were our special days
Bright with love,
Resounding with laughter,
High days, holidays,
Days when we took time:
Time to be together,
To share and celebrate.

Memories of childhood

His *age*

Place

Her *age*

Place

Other memorable holidays

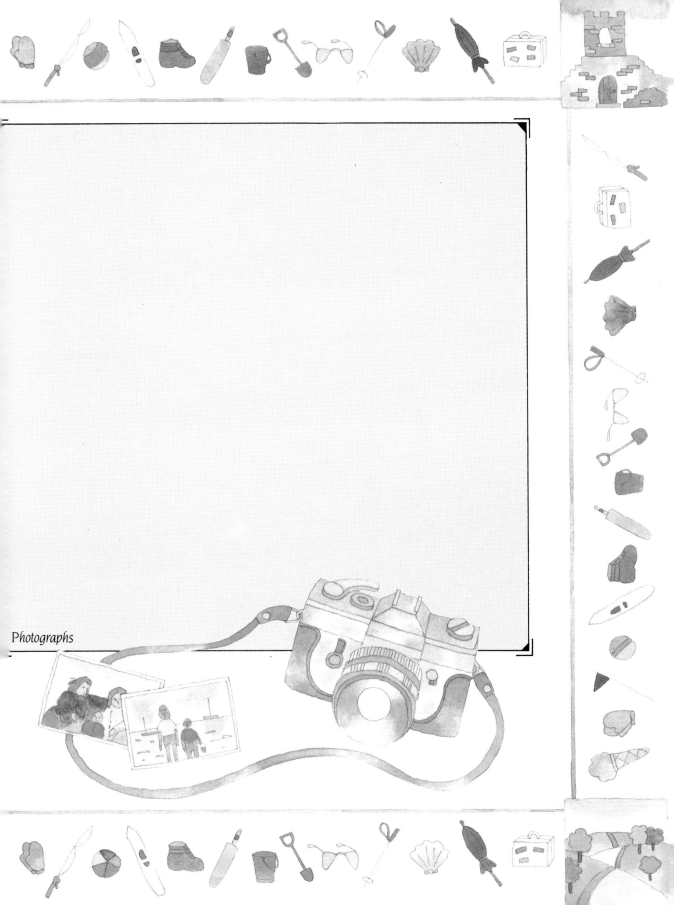

Photographs

WIT WISDOM AND MEMORABLE MOMENTS

My grandfather once told me that there are two kinds of people.

Those who do the work

and those who take the credit.

He told me to try to be in the first group

There was much less competition there.

Indira Gandhi

Family sayings

Memorable moments

Awful incidents

Memorable moments

Family sayings

Memorable moments

Awful incidents

Family sayings

THE CIRCLE WIDENS — WEDDINGS

And so the circle widens
A birth, a marriage,
Fresh faces, new ideas.
We welcome you
With open arms.
For you are someone special,
And your coming
Adds something very precious
To our lives.

Name of newly married couple

Relationship to us (if any)

Date and place of wedding

Who was there

Name of newly married couple

Relationship to us (if any)

Date and place of wedding

Who was there

Name of newly married couple

Relationship to us (if any)

Date and place of wedding

Who was there

Name of newly married couple

Relationship to us (if any)

Date and place of wedding

Who was there

Name of newly married couple

Relationship to us (if any)

Date and place of wedding

Who was there

Name of newly married couple

Relationship to us (if any)

Date and place of wedding

Who was there

M E M O R I E S

Life itself is a gift from God
Presented to us in morning-fresh wrappings
One day at a time.
It can be spent, wasted or invested
But once gone, no day can be re-lived
Nor can we take a time loan
From the future.
And it is largely in our own hands
Whether the sum of our days
Will become an empty shell of opportunities lost
Or a life-work complete —
Something beautiful for God.

Memories of childhood

How we celebrated Christmas

Family outings remembered

Memories of childhood

Other special moments

Other special moments

39

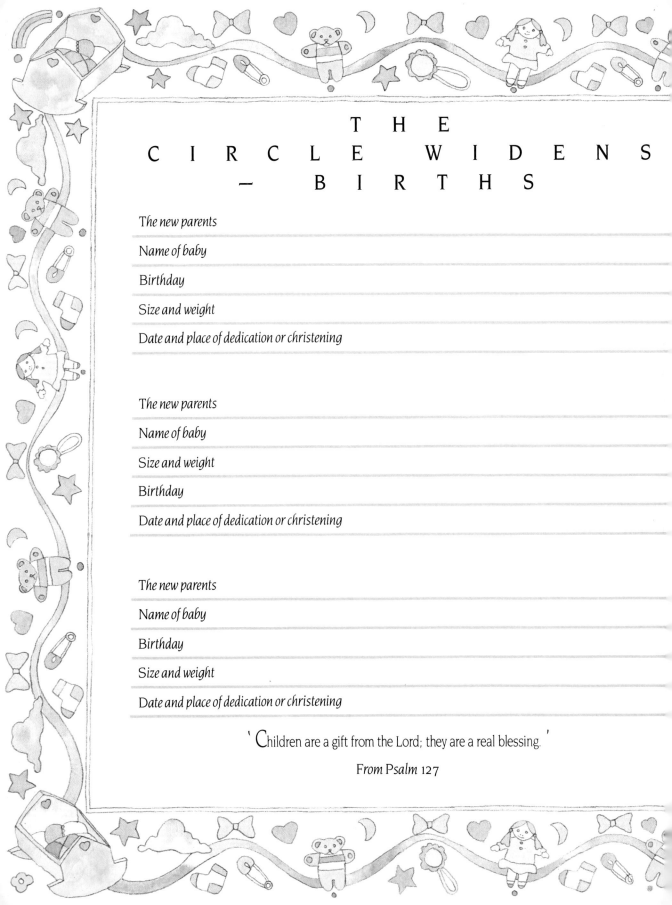

THE CIRCLE WIDENS – BIRTHS

The new parents
_____

Name of baby
_____

Birthday
_____

Size and weight
_____

Date and place of dedication or christening
_____

The new parents
_____

Name of baby
_____

Size and weight
_____

Birthday
_____

Date and place of dedication or christening
_____

The new parents
_____

Name of baby
_____

Birthday
_____

Size and weight
_____

Date and place of dedication or christening
_____

'Children are a gift from the Lord; they are a real blessing.'

From Psalm 127

The new parents

Name of baby

Birthday

Size and weight

Date and place of dedication or christening

The new parents

Name of baby

Birthday

Size and weight

Date and place of dedication or christening

The new parents

Name of baby

Birthday

Size and weight

Date and place of dedication or christening

Sports certificates or cups

_____
_____
_____
_____
_____
_____

Qualifications obtained

_____
_____
_____
_____
_____
_____

Competitions or performances

_____
_____
_____
_____
_____
_____

Newspaper cuttings

Details of telegrams

T E S T I N G   T I M E S

Family bereavements

Name   Date
_____

Name   Date
_____

Name   Date
_____

Name   Date
_____

Name   Date
_____

Other crises or times of difficulty
_____

_____

_____

_____

_____

_____

_____

These words have helped in times of need...
_____

_____

_____

'Come to me, all you who are weary and burdened,
and I will give you rest.'
The words of Jesus, in Matthew's Gospel, chapter 11

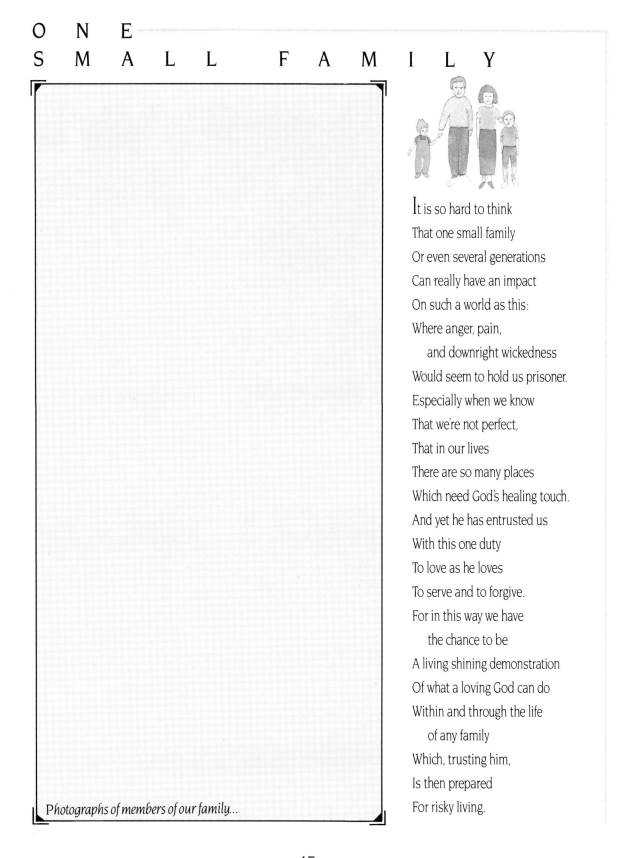

Photographs of members of our family...

It is so hard to think
That one small family
Or even several generations
Can really have an impact
On such a world as this:
Where anger, pain,
   and downright wickedness
Would seem to hold us prisoner.
Especially when we know
That we're not perfect,
That in our lives
There are so many places
Which need God's healing touch.
And yet he has entrusted us
With this one duty
To love as he loves
To serve and to forgive.
For in this way we have
   the chance to be
A living shining demonstration
Of what a loving God can do
Within and through the life
   of any family
Which, trusting him,
Is then prepared
For risky living.